A World of
Toys and Games

Susie Williams

W
FRANKLIN WATTS
LONDON • SYDNEY

First published in Great Britain in 2025 by Hodder & Stoughton
Copyright © Hodder & Stoughton Limited, 2025
All rights reserved.

Credits
Editor: Victoria Brooker
Designer: Rocket Design (East Anglia) Ltd

Picture credits:
Alamy: Westend61 GmbH:23b.
Shutterstock: Africa Studio 29, alexmisu f cover cal, 1cl, 4tc, 30tr; Johanna Altmann 17t;
Avtk 7;Ilia Bliznyuk 12r; Brulove 25cl, 32tr; Alesandra Budnik 15b;Jesus Cervantes 10b;
AJCespedes 13t; Clones f cover bl,1bcl, 4bl, 30tl; Conzorb 20cb; Daniid 15t;
Chirag Dave 24b; G Evgenij 18b; Ezume Images 21b; Favepng f cover br, 1c, 5br, 6b;
Fh Photo 27br; Flowerino 8b; BW Folsom 31tr; GrashAlex 26t; Margo Harrison 9b;
iceink 9t; IfiStudio f cover bc, 4-5b,32b; Jorgerayagarcia 3br, 24c; Krotnakro 16t;
Yaroslav Kryuchka 2, 13br; Sergiy Kuzmin 19b; Lenorko 27t; Sreeyash Lohiya 16b;
Mallika Maharjan 22b; Malachy666 20c; Linda McKenna 6cl;Melicaf cover clc, 1tc, 4cr;
Mulad Images 11b; Mumum96 17b; New Africa f cover l,cr, 1cr, 1bl, 4c, 5cl,18t,
23t, 25cr, 28, 32tl; SrdrOzsoy 14b; Photo Melon 3tr, 22t; Pixel Shot 25br;
Dawn Quadling 21t; Reflex Life 11t; Elena Schweitzer 27cl, 27bl; Noey Smiley 3bl, 25t;
Squeeb Creative 10t; StockingImageFactory 19r; StockSimo 20b;
Tatyaby 3bl; Charles Taylor 12l;Tenacity_1987 f cover cacl; 4tcr; Timmary 26b;
Evgeniya Tiplyasgina 24l, 30b; Tanveer Anjum Towsif f cover c, 1tr; 5cl; 2017 lightrain 19tl;
Ubanbuzz 14t; Valentin Valkov f cover ca,1tl, 3cl,5tl, 8t; Peter Vanco 3tl, 7tl; Yarrbush 3cr, 20t.

Every attempt has been made to clear copyright. Should there be any inadvertent omission please apply to the publisher for rectification.

HB ISBN: 978 1 4451 9642 8
PB ISBN: 978 1 4451 9644 2
EBK ISBN: 978 1 4451 9643 5

Printed in Dubai

Franklin Watts
An imprint of
Hachette Children's Group
Part of Hodder & Stoughton
Carmelite House
50 Victoria Embankment
London EC4Y 0DZ

An Hachette UK Company
www.hachette.co.uk

www.hachettechildrens.co.uk

The authorised representative in the EEA is Hachette Ireland,
8 Castlecourt Centre, Dublin 15, D15 XTP3, Ireland (email: info@hbgi.ie)

We strongly advise that Internet access is supervised by a responsible adult. The website addresses (URLs) included in this book were valid at the time of going to press. However, it is possible that contents or addresses may have changed since the publication of this book. No responsibility for any such changes can be accepted by either the author or the Publisher.

CONTENTS

Toys and games for everyone! 4
Cuddly toys 6
Dolls 8
Toys that move 10
Robots 12
Transport toys 14
Puppets 16
Outdoor toys and games 18
Board games 20
Flying toys 22
Get creative 24
Musical toys 26
Make a sock puppet 28
Glossary 30
Further information 31
Index 32

Toys and Games

What's your favourite toy? What games do you like to play? Every day, around the world, children like to play with their favourite toys and games, too. Right now, there will be someone skipping, or playing with cars, or cuddling a toy.

Learn how to make me on page 28.

FOR EVERYONE!

Let's find out about the toys and games that children love to play with, now and in the past.

CUDDLY TOYS

The first teddy was made in the USA in 1903. It was named after the American president, Teddy Roosevelt. Old teddy bears were often made from animal fur. They were stuffed with wood shavings or straw.

Old teddy bears were not always very cuddly!

Soon, other animals were made into stuffed creatures too. Cuddly toys come in many different colours and shapes. You can have cuddly giraffes, seahorses or ice creams!

DOLLS

Children have been playing with dolls for hundreds of years. In the past, dolls were made from wood, china or cloth. Most dolls today are made from plastic. Some dolls can even cry or talk to you!

Dolls are made in lots of different sizes and types.

In Japan, Kokeshi dolls are made from wood and painted. They have no arms or legs. Kokeshi dolls are said to bring good luck and are often given as a gift.

In the past, in Germany and the Netherlands, dolls' houses were not toys but were bought by adults. Only later did they become a children's toy.

Toys that move

Toys that move are great fun to watch. Spinning tops work by pushing a lever up and down to make them spin.

These wooden spinning toys are called *trompos* in Mexico. You pull the string to make the top spin. There are similar toys to these all over the world. These toys were also played with long ago in ancient Egypt and ancient Greece.

For centuries, around the world, rocking horses have been popular. They can be decorated in beautiful colours and designs. In China, traditional rocking horses were made from wood and bamboo.

Nowadays, toys have batteries that make them move. This remote-controlled car can zoom along using hand-held controls.

ROBOTS

Toy robots from the 1950s were made to move by clockwork. A key wound up the clockwork machinery inside. The robot would then start to walk.

GREETINGS!

Later, robots had flashing lights and sounds.

These days, robots can move quickly, talk to you and help you. You can have robotic cars, dogs and even drones.

13

TRANSPORT TOYS

It's fun to make toys zoom along. On water, plastic or wooden boats easily float.

These sailing boats have been made from walnut shells. You can have a race and blow the sail of your boat to make it move.

Railway sets have been popular for more than 100 years. Wooden trains can be moved by hand. Metal trains use batteries to help them move.

Tracks can be plastic, wood or metal and can be as small or large as you have space for! You can add stations, buildings, trees and tunnels to make the journey more exciting.

PUPPETS

A family of finger puppets.

People use puppets to make up stories or retell familiar tales.

In India, *Kathputli* puppets dance about on strings. You have to be careful not to get them tangled!

In Indonesia, children move shadow puppets on sticks to put on a play.

Wayang Potehi hand puppets in China are made of paper or leather. They can be used to perform a traditional Chinese opera.

Outdoor Toys and Games

Hopscotch is an easy and fun game to play outside. Using chalk, you draw a number grid and hop along it. You throw a stone or marker into one square and then you have to hop around it – without falling over!

In France and some other countries, there is a circular hopscotch game called *escargot*, which means 'snail' in French. Can you see why it is called that?

Can you keep a hula hoop spinning? These days most are made with plastic, but in the past they were made from metal or wood. Do you think that would have made them harder or easier to use?

Can you think of any other toys you can play with outside?

BOARD GAMES

Board games are fun to play on a rainy day. There are lots to choose from. Common ones such as snakes and ladders, ludo, backgammon and chess are played by children and adults all over the world.

Ludo

Backgammon

Chess uses special pieces called chessmen.

First invented in India, snakes and ladders is now played in many countries.

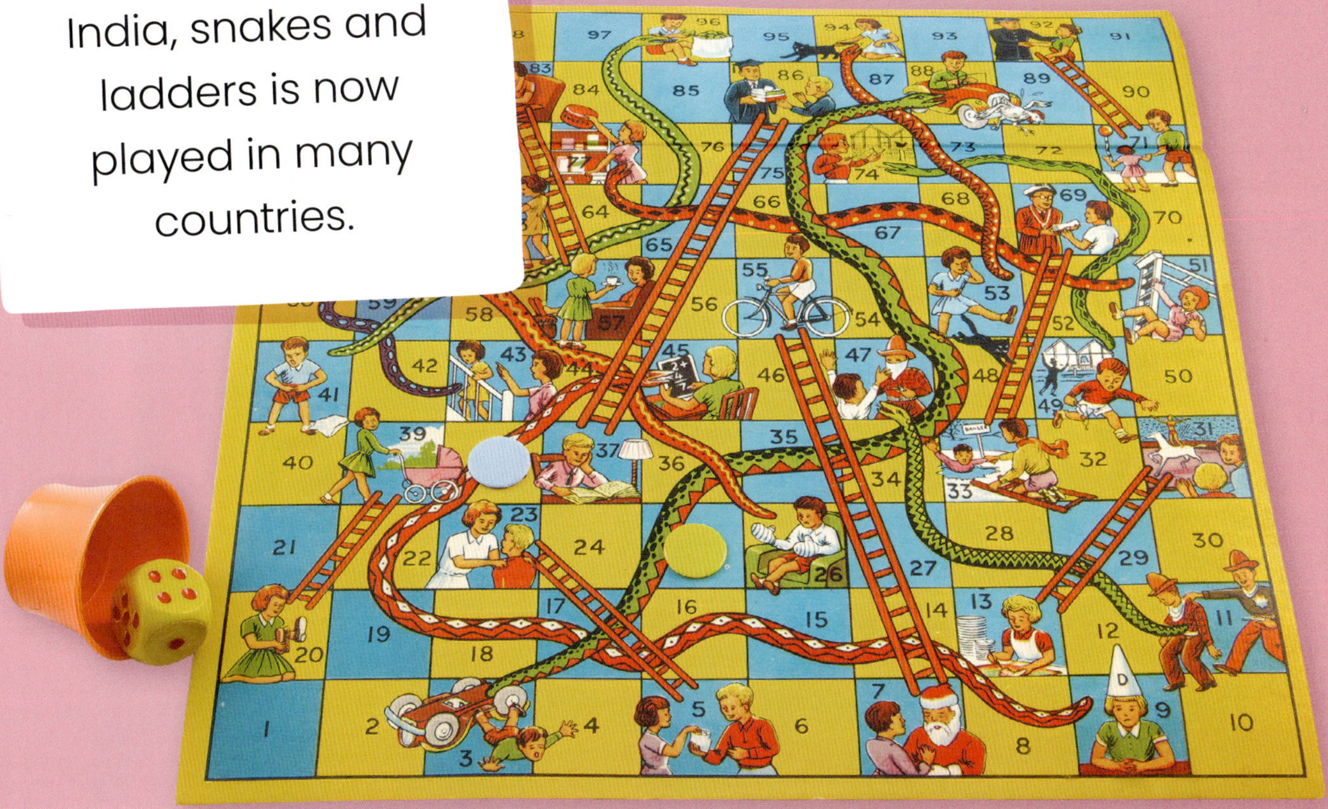

Glass marbles can be used in modern bao games.

Bao is a traditional game played in most of Africa, which has also spread around the world. This ancient game is played with small stones or seeds.

FLYING TOYS

Soaring in the air, kites dip and swoop on the breeze. Kites can be different shapes and sizes. You can buy them or make your own.

Many countries have kite flying festivals. Look at these kites flying at a festival in Adelaide, Australia.

Frisbees, or flying discs, are flat toys that are flown through the air for a friend to catch. They were invented in the United States in the 1930s.

Toy aeroplanes are great fun to play with. You can make your own with model kits or simply just fold a piece of paper into a plane shape to fly. People also fly toy drones.

GET CREATIVE

Everyone loves to get creative with pens, paper and paint. Whether drawing a picture, painting some pebbles or colouring in a pattern, it's a fun way to express yourself.

This rangoli pattern has been painted outside to celebrate a Hindu festival.

Modelling clay is great to knead and shape. You can mould it into anything you like. People have been making things with clay for thousands of years. Not only is it fun to play with, you can make useful things, such as bowls or pots, with it, too.

Origami is the Japanese art of folding paper into different shapes. Origami comes from two Japanese words – *ori* which means folding and *kami* which means paper. Have you ever tried to do it?

MUSICAL TOYS

Maracas are traditionally from South and Central America. They were first made from wood and filled with seeds or pebbles. These days, they can be made from plastic or metal, too. You shake them to make a sound.

Jingles

Tambourines have disc-shapes called 'jingles' around the frame. You can shake, hit or rub them to make a noise.

Drums are fun to tap out a beat on. The *djembe* is an African drum that can be played using your whole hand or just your fingers.

What other musical instruments can you play?

Make a Sock Puppet

I'm ready to play!

You will need:
- An old sock
- Cotton wool
- Googly eyes or buttons
- Glue
- Wool

Instructions

1 Ask an adult to help you glue some strands of wool on to the sock for the hair. You could plait the hair before you glue it, or make it long or short.

2 Then glue the googly eyes on to the cotton wool. Glue the cotton wool eyes on to the sock.

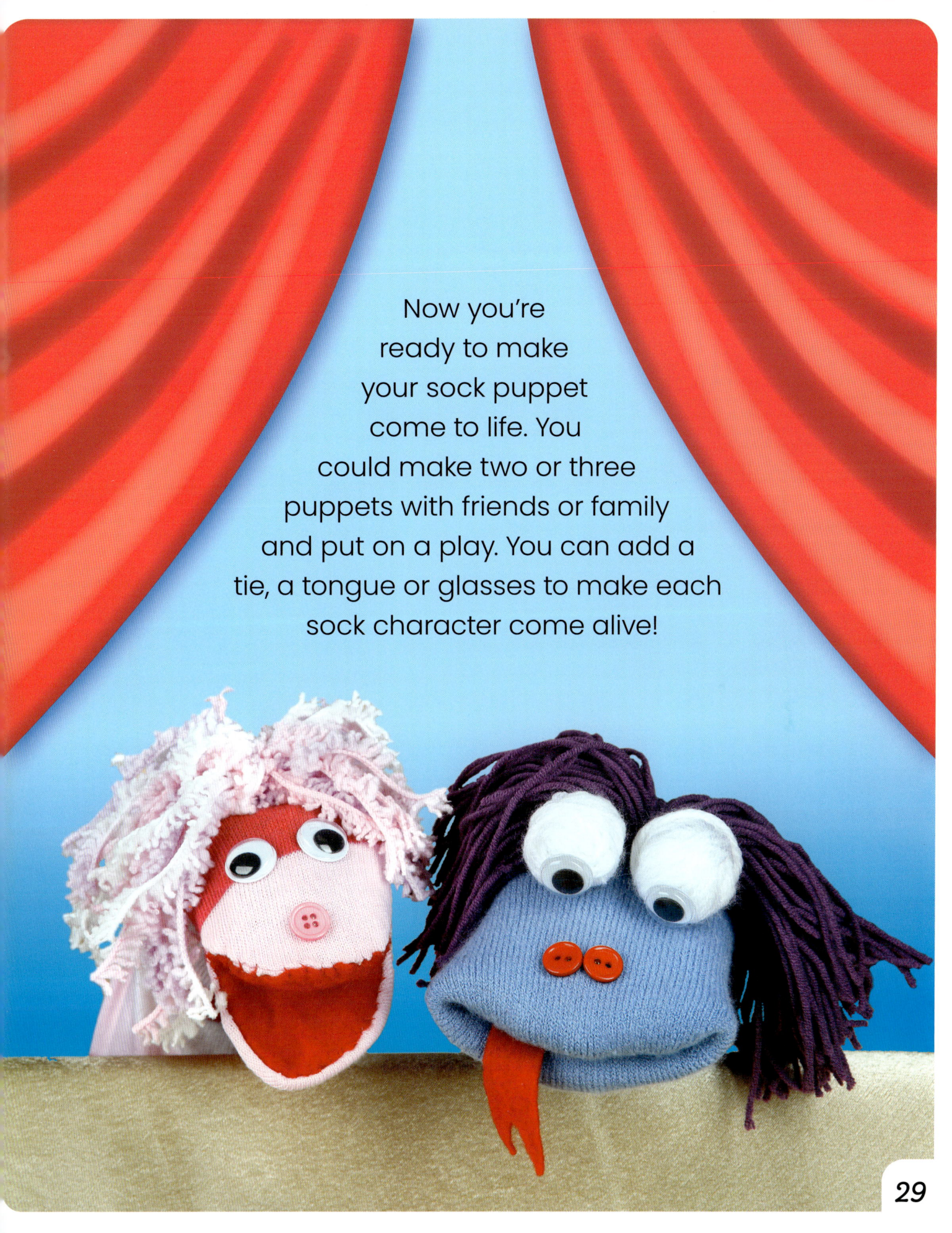

Now you're ready to make your sock puppet come to life. You could make two or three puppets with friends or family and put on a play. You can add a tie, a tongue or glasses to make each sock character come alive!

Glossary

ancient very old

bamboo a tall, grass plant that has hard, woody, hollow stalks

battery a device that stores energy until it is needed

clockwork a machine containing a set of small cogwheels to make something move

drone a device that flies using a remote control

lever a tool used to move things

mould to shape something

opera a play in which all or most of the words are sung

rangoli a traditional Hindu decoration on a floor

remote controlled the control of a machine from a distance

Further Information

BOOKS ABOUT TOYS

Dogger by Shirley Hughes

I Love You, Blue Kangaroo by Emma Chichester Clark

Lost in the Toy Museum by David Lucas

Stanley's Stick by John Hegley

Tatty Ratty by Helen Cooper

That Rabbit Belongs to Emily Brown by Cressida Cowell and Neal Layton

Toys in Space by Mini Grey

Ways Into History: Toys and Games by Sally Hewitt

WEBSITES

Find out about toys and games from 100 years ago:
www.bbc.co.uk/bitesize/articles/z8x7m39

Visit some fantastic museums to see lots of different toys and games:

www.pollockstoymuseum.co.uk/

www.brightontoymuseum.co.uk/

www.edinburghmuseums.org.uk/venue/museum-childhood

www.museumslondon.org/museum/143/v-a-museum-of-childhood

www.ilkleytoymuseum.co.uk/

www.yorkcastlemuseum.org.uk/exhibition/mechanical-marvels/

INDEX

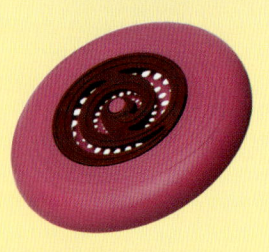

aeroplanes 23

backgammon 20
bicycle 19
board games 20–21
boats 14

cars 4, 11, 13
cuddly toys 6–7

dolls 8–9
  Kokeshi dolls 9
dolls' houses 9
drones 13, 23
drums 27

flying toys 22–23
frisbees 23

hula hoop 19
hopscotch 18

kites 22
  kite festival, Australia 22
ludo 20

maracas 26
modelling clay 25
musical toys 26–27

origami 25
outdoor toys and games 18–19

painting 24
puppets 16–17, 28–29

robots 12–13
rocking horse 11

skipping 4
snakes and ladders 20, 21
spinning tops 10

tambourines 26
teddy bears 6, 7
toys that move 10–11
trains 15
transport toys 14–15